One-Yard Sewin

50 Fun and Easy Patterns to Transform Small Cuts of Fabric into Stylish Creations

Angelica J. Anderson

TABLE OF CONTENT

Chapter One 5

Getting Started with One-Yard Sewing 5

Chapter Two 9

Quick & Easy Accessories 9

Chapter Three.............19

Home & Living 19

Chapter Four.............29

For the Kitchen 29

Chapter Five.............37

Fashion Fun 37

Chapter Six.............45

Gifts & Celebrations 45

Chapter Seven 53

Kids & Play.............53

Chapter Eight 61

Eco-Friendly Sewing 61

Chapter Nine 69

Seasonal & Holiday Projects.............69

Chapter Ten 76

Upcycling & Creative Remixes...........77

Chapter Eleven 86

Finishing Touches & Personalization.................86

Chapter Twelve...............................93

Sewing Tips for Every Skill Level.......93

Conclusion 98

Your One-Yard Sewing Journey 98

CHAPTER ONE

Getting Started with One-Yard Sewing

Sewing Tools & Supplies Checklist

Choosing the Right Fabrics for Different Projects

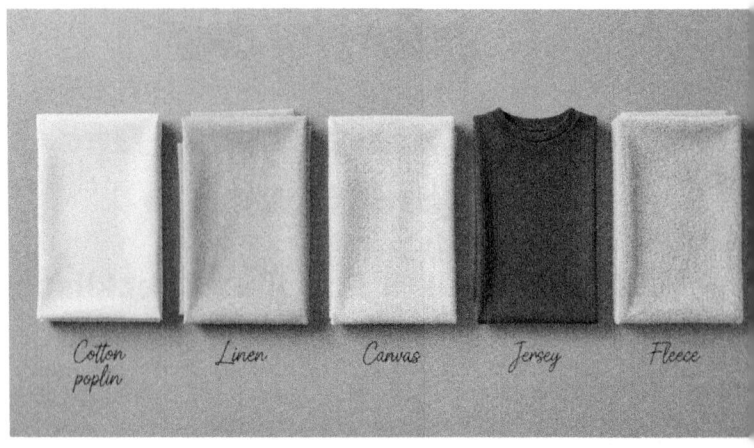

Cotton poplin   Linen   Canvas   Jersey   Fleece

- fabric weights (lightweight, medium, heavyweight).
- Best fabrics for accessories, home décor, kids' projects, etc.
- Swatches of different fabric types (cotton, linen, canvas, jersey, fleece).
- Side-by-side comparison showing lightweight cotton vs. heavyweight denim.

Basic Stitches and Techniques You'll Use Throughout This Book

- Straight stitch, zigzag stitch, backstitch.
- Simple seam finishes (pinked edge, zigzag edge, French seam).
- Pressing seams open with an iron.

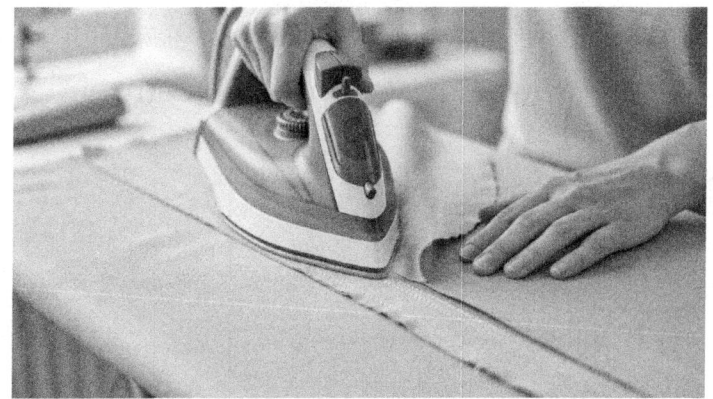

- Sewing machine stitching fabric with arrows indicating stitch direction.
- A visual chart of different stitch types side by side.
- Step photos: sewing a seam → trimming → pressing it open.

Tips for Sewing Success (Pressing, Finishing Seams, Troubleshooting)

- Pressing is as important as sewing.
- Preventing frayed edges with finishing techniques.
- Iron pressing a seam on an ironing board.
- Before/after images of unfinished raw edge vs. finished seam.

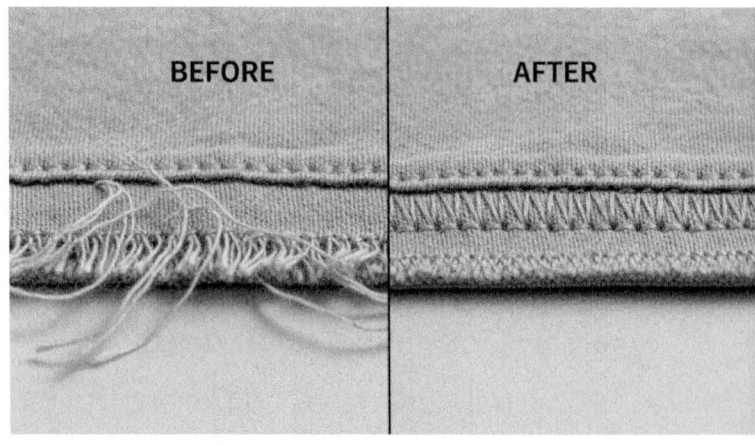

CHAPTER TWO

Quick & Easy Accessories

Accessories are the perfect way to start with one-yard projects. They're practical, stylish, and easy to personalize. In this chapter, you'll find five simple projects that use minimal fabric but give maximum results.

Project 1: Tote Bag

Fabric Suggestions: Medium-weight cotton, canvas, denim, or linen. **Variations:** Add a lining, pockets, or decorative trims.

Steps:

1. Cut two rectangles of fabric (approx. 16" x 14").
2. Cut two strips (20" x 3") for handles.
3. Sew side and bottom seams of the rectangles.
4. Hem the top edge by folding twice and stitching.
5. Sew handles in place securely.

Project 2: Drawstring Backpack

Fabric Suggestions: Quilting cotton, canvas, or lightweight denim.

Variations: Use contrasting fabric for casing or add an appliqué.

Steps:

1. Cut two fabric rectangles (16" x 18").
2. Sew side seams and bottom seam, leaving openings for the drawstring casing.
3. Fold the top edge to make a casing. Stitch.
4. Insert cord or ribbon through casing and thread through the bottom corners.
5. Knot ends securely to form straps.

Project 3: Headbands

Fabric Suggestions: Knit fabric, cotton, or silky fabrics for a dressy version.

Variations: Add elastic for adjustable fit, twist style, or bow detail.

Steps:

1. Cut a strip of fabric (20" x 6").
2. Fold lengthwise, right sides together, and stitch along the long edge.
3. Turn tube right side out.
4. Fold raw edges inward and topstitch closed.
5. Optional: Add a short piece of elastic at the back for stretch.

Project 4: Zipper Pouch

Fabric Suggestions: Quilting cotton, canvas, or linen (light interfacing recommended).

Variations: Try patchwork, embroidery, or contrast lining.

Steps:

1. Cut two fabric rectangles (9" x 6") and two lining pieces of same size.
2. Place fabric and zipper right sides together, stitch. Repeat with other side.
3. Fold pouch right sides together, sew sides and bottom.
4. Turn right side out, press neatly.

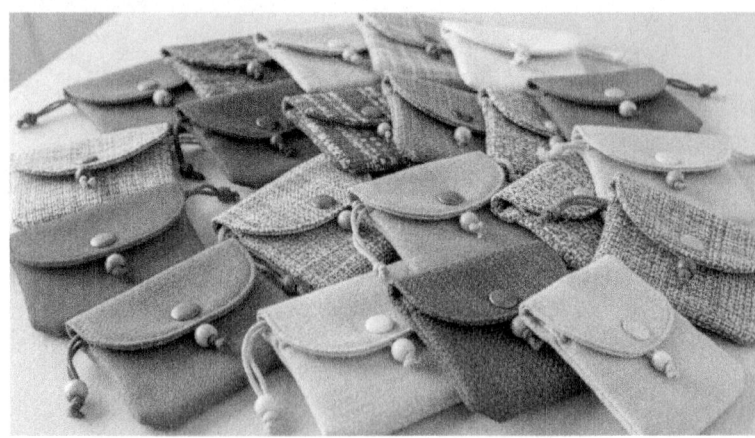

Project 5: Fabric Belt

Fabric Suggestions: Cotton, twill, or linen. Interfacing for sturdiness. **Variations:** Make reversible with two fabrics, add decorative stitching.

Steps:

1. Cut a strip of fabric (length = waist + 20", width = 4").
2. Fold in half lengthwise, stitch long side, turn right side out.

3. Press and topstitch edges for a neat finish.

4. Thread belt through a D-ring buckle or tie ends into a bow.

CHAPTER THREE

Home & Living

Home décor projects are some of the most rewarding one-yard sewing ideas. They transform everyday living spaces into something fresh and personal, while also being beginner-friendly. With just a yard of fabric, you can brighten your home, stay organized, and add handmade charm to your kitchen or dining table.

Project 1: Throw Pillow Cover

Fabric Suggestions: Quilting cotton, linen, canvas, or decorator fabric. **Variations:** Add piping, tassels, or an appliqué design.

Steps:

1. Cut one piece of fabric 18" x 18" for the pillow front.
2. Cut two pieces 18" x 12" for the envelope-style back.
3. Hem one long edge on each back piece.

4. Place front and back pieces right sides together, overlapping the backs.

5. Stitch around all four sides. Turn right side out. Insert pillow form.

Project 2: Fabric Storage Baskets

Fabric Suggestions: Sturdy cotton, canvas, denim, or duck cloth. Use interfacing for structure. **Variations:** Add handles, make reversible, or sew in multiple sizes.

Steps:

1. Cut two rectangles of fabric (14" x 18") and two lining pieces of the same size.
2. Place fabric and lining right sides together, stitch side seams.

3. Box the corners by folding and stitching across bottom corners.

4. Insert lining into outer basket, fold top edges inward, and stitch.

5. Turn down the top cuff for a finished look.

Project 3: Apron

Fabric Suggestions: Cotton, denim, twill, or linen.

Variations: Add a pocket, ruffles, or a contrasting waistband.

Steps:

1. Cut apron body (28" x 20"). Cut one waistband strip (36" x 4") and two neck ties (20" x 2").
2. Hem the apron's raw edges.
3. Attach waistband and ties to top edge of apron.

4. Sew pocket piece (optional 8" x 8") onto the front.

5. Press all edges neatly for a crisp finish.

Project 4: Kitchen Towel with Decorative Trim

Fabric   Suggestions: Absorbent cotton, linen, or waffle-weave fabric. **Variations:**   Add   rickrack,   lace, appliqué, or embroidered details.

Steps:

1. Cut one rectangle 18" x 28".
2. Hem all four edges by folding ½" twice and stitching.
3. Add decorative trim to one short edge (rickrack, lace, or ribbon).
4. Press towel for a polished finish.

Project 5: Table Runner

Fabric Suggestions: Cotton, linen, canvas, or quilting cotton. **Variations:** Add patchwork, tassels, or quilted batting for thickness.

Steps:

1. Cut one piece 14" x 36".

2. Hem all edges neatly or add a contrasting fabric backing.

3. Optional: Stitch batting between layers for a quilted effect.

4. Add tassels or fringe to the short edges if desired.

CHAPTER FOUR

For the Kitchen

The kitchen is the heart of the home, and handmade fabric projects make it even warmer and more inviting. With just a yard of fabric, you can create eco-friendly items, practical tools, and decorative accents that make cooking and entertaining more enjoyable.

Project 1: Reusable Snack Bags

Fabric Suggestions: Quilting cotton (outer) + food-safe lining such as PUL or nylon.

Variations: Add Velcro, snaps, or zipper closures. Make in multiple sizes for sandwiches or snacks.

Steps:

1. Cut one piece of outer fabric and one piece of lining (7" x 6").
2. Place right sides together, stitch sides and bottom, leaving top open.
3. Turn right side out and press.
4. Fold top edge inward, insert closure (Velcro, snap, or zipper).
5. Stitch along the top to secure.

Project 2: Wine Bottle Bag

Fabric Suggestions: Cotton, linen, or canvas.

Variations: Add a contrasting lining, ribbon tie, or decorative trim.

Steps:

1. Cut fabric rectangle 16" x 20".
2. Fold in half lengthwise, right sides together, and stitch side seam.
3. Stitch across the bottom to close.

4. Optional: Box the corners for a flat bottom.

5. Fold top edge down ½" twice and stitch for a neat hem.

6. Tie with ribbon, rope, or a fabric strip.

Project 3: Oven Mitt

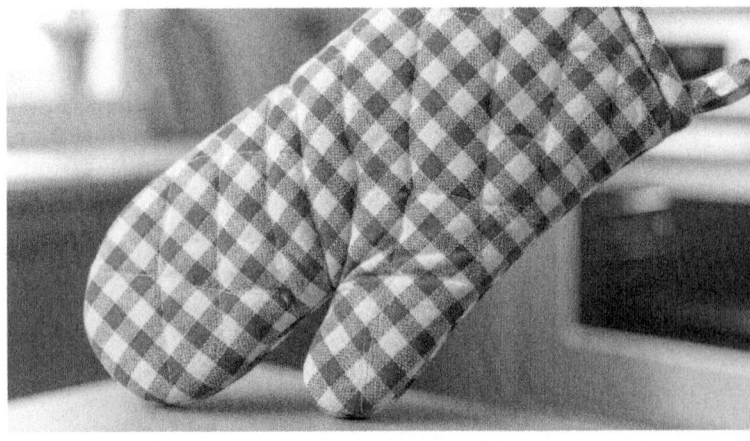

Fabric Suggestions: Quilting cotton with heat-resistant batting (like Insul-Bright). Lining in cotton.

Variations: Add hanging loop, use patchwork, or quilted stitching.

Steps:

1. Cut two outer fabric pieces and two lining pieces using a mitt template.
2. Cut two batting pieces the same size.
3. Layer outer fabric + batting + lining. Quilt through layers.
4. Place two quilted pieces right sides together, stitch around edge, leaving wrist open.
5. Turn right side out, hem wrist edge, and add loop if desired.

Project 4: Pot Holders

Fabric Suggestions: Cotton fabric, cotton batting, or heat-resistant batting.

Variations: Add pocket for hand slip-in, try patchwork designs, or use decorative quilting.

Steps:

1. Cut two 8" x 8" fabric squares and one batting square of same size.

2. Layer fabric right side down, batting, then fabric right side up.

3. Quilt across all layers in straight or diagonal lines.

4. Bind edges with bias tape, leaving a small loop in one corner.

Project 5: Bread Basket Liner

Fabric Suggestions: Cotton, linen, or muslin.

Variations: Add embroidery, lace trim, or reversible fabric.

Steps:

1. Cut fabric square 20" x 20".
2. Hem all four sides with a narrow double fold.
3. Optional: Add lace or ribbon trim around the edges.
4. Place inside bread basket with corners draping over.

CHAPTER FIVE

Fashion Fun

Fashion projects are some of the most exciting one-yard creations because they let you wear your work proudly. With simple cuts and easy sewing techniques, you can transform fabric into stylish garments and accessories that look boutique-made but are budget-friendly and quick to sew.

Project 1: Infinity Scarf

Fabric Suggestions: Lightweight cotton, voile, rayon, jersey knit, or chiffon.

Variations: Make it double-layered for warmth, add lace trim, or create a twisted version.

Steps:

1. Cut fabric rectangle 60" x 20" (or use the full fabric width).
2. Fold in half lengthwise, right sides together, and stitch long edge.
3. Turn tube right side out.
4. Join short ends together, stitch closed neatly.
5. Press for a smooth finish.

Project 2: Kimono-Style Jacket

Fabric Suggestions: Lightweight cotton, rayon, voile, or chiffon. **Variations:** Add lace trim to sleeves, shorten for a shrug, or make longer for a robe-style.

Steps:

1. Cut fabric rectangle 36" x 44". Fold in half lengthwise.
2. Cut a straight line up the center front to create opening.

3. Cut shallow curves for sleeves at the fold edge.

4. Hem all raw edges with a narrow double fold.

5. Optional: Add trim along sleeves and hem.

Project 3: Wrap Skirt

Fabric Suggestions: Cotton, linen, chambray, or rayon.

Variations: Add a ruffle hem, make reversible, or shorten for a mini version.

Steps:

1. Cut rectangle 45" x 30".

2. Hem all edges.

3. Cut two long strips (36" x 3") for waist ties.

4. Attach ties securely to top corners of fabric.

5. Wrap around waist and tie at side.

Project 4: Simple Tunic Top

Fabric Suggestions: Cotton lawn, rayon, voile, or light linen.

Variations: Add trim at neckline, belt at waist, or make sleeveless.

Steps:

1. Cut two rectangles 20" x 28".
2. Place right sides together, stitch sides, leaving 8" open at top for armholes.
3. Stitch shoulders, leaving 8–10" opening at center for neckline.
4. Hem armholes, neckline, and bottom edges.
5. Optional: Add side slits for movement.

Project 5: Fabric Clutch

Fabric Suggestions: Cotton canvas, denim, or faux leather with interfacing for sturdiness.

Variations: Add zipper closure, magnetic snap, or wrist strap.

Steps:

1. Cut two fabric rectangles 12" x 8" and two lining pieces.

2. Apply fusible interfacing to outer pieces for structure.

3. Place outer and lining pieces right sides together, stitch around edges, leaving top open.

4. Insert zipper or fold-over flap for closure.

5. Press and topstitch edges for a neat look.

CHAPTER SIX

Gifts & Celebrations

Handmade gifts always carry a special meaning, and one-yard sewing projects make it simple to create thoughtful treasures for loved ones. Whether it's a birthday, holiday, or baby shower, these quick projects are both useful and heartfelt.

Project 1: Gift Bags

Fabric Suggestions: Quilting cotton, linen, canvas, or festive prints. **Variations:** Add ribbon drawstrings, appliqué initials, or make them reversible.

Steps:

1. Cut fabric rectangle 14" x 18".
2. Fold in half, right sides together, and stitch side and bottom seams.
3. Fold top edge down ½" twice to create casing. Stitch close to fold.
4. Thread ribbon or cord through casing using a safety pin.
5. Knot ends and pull tight to close.

Project 2: Fabric Bookmarks

Fabric Suggestions: Quilting cotton, linen, or scraps with interfacing. **Variations:** Add embroidery, tassels, or make patchwork designs.

Steps:

1. Cut fabric strip 8" x 2". Cut interfacing same size.
2. Fuse interfacing to fabric for stability.

3. Fold edges inward, stitch around all sides neatly.

4. Optional: Sew ribbon or tassel at the top.

Project 3: Jewelry Roll Organizer

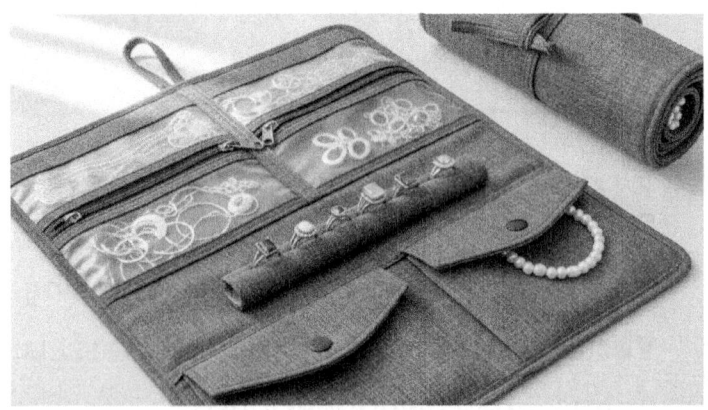

Fabric Suggestions: Cotton, silk, or satin with lightweight interfacing. **Variations:** Add pockets for earrings, ring holder strips, or quilted padding.

Steps:

1. Cut outer fabric rectangle 12" x 18", lining same size, and batting if desired.

2. Cut smaller pocket pieces (various sizes). Hem their top edges.

3. Arrange pockets on lining, stitch sides and bottoms.

4. Place outer fabric and lining right sides together, stitch around edges, leaving opening.

5. Turn right side out, press, and stitch opening closed.

6. Add ribbon ties to close roll.

Project 4: Travel Shoe Bag

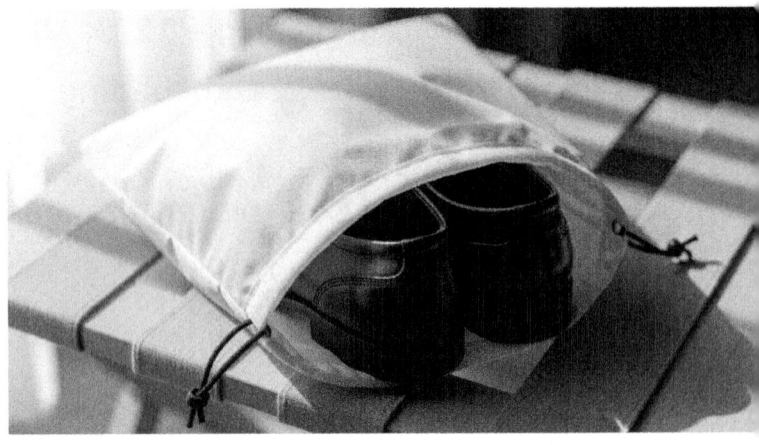

Fabric Suggestions: Cotton, canvas, or nylon.

Variations: Make drawstring or zipper version; embroider monogram initials.

Steps:

1. Cut two fabric rectangles 16" x 20".
2. Place right sides together, stitch sides and bottom.
3. Hem top edge or sew casing for drawstring.

4. Thread cord or ribbon through casing.

5. Optional: Add divider seam down the middle to separate shoes.

Project 5: Baby Bibs

Fabric Suggestions: Soft cotton, terry cloth, or flannel. Lining optional for absorbency.

Variations: Add snap or Velcro closure, applique animals, or patchwork designs.

Steps:

1. Cut two bib shapes from fabric using a template.
2. Place right sides together, stitch around edges, leaving neck opening.
3. Clip curves, turn right side out, and press.
4. Topstitch around bib for durability.
5. Attach Velcro or snap at neck closure.

CHAPTER SEVEN

Kids & Play

Children love handmade treasures, and sewing with just one yard of fabric opens up endless possibilities for toys, dress-up fun, and creative playtime. These projects are simple, safe, and perfect for gifting or making alongside kids to introduce them to sewing.

Project 1: Stuffed Animal

Fabric Suggestions: Soft cotton, flannel, fleece, or felt.

Variations: Make different shapes (bear, bunny, cat, or elephant), add simple embroidery for features instead of buttons for safety.

Steps:

1. Draw or trace an animal shape onto paper to use as a pattern.
2. Cut two fabric pieces from the pattern.
3. Place right sides together, stitch around edges, leaving a small opening.
4. Clip curves and turn right side out.
5. Stuff with polyfill and stitch opening closed.

Project 2: Doll Clothes

Fabric Suggestions: Cotton scraps, flannel, or knit fabric for stretch.

Variations: Make a simple dress,

pants, or skirt; add Velcro for easy closures.

Steps:

1. Measure doll or use simple templates for doll-sized clothing.
2. Cut fabric pieces according to chosen design.
3. Sew side seams and hems.
4. Add Velcro or snaps for back closure.
5. Embellish with ribbon, lace, or trim.

Project 3: Child's Apron

Fabric Suggestions: Cotton, denim, or canvas.

Variations: Add a pocket, make reversible, or decorate with fabric paint.

Steps:

1. Cut apron body (18" x 22").

2. Cut one waistband strip (24" x 3") and two neck ties (18" x 2").

3. Hem apron edges.

4. Attach waistband and ties.

5. Optional: Add a front pocket (8" x 6").

Project 4: Fabric Crown

Fabric Suggestions: Cotton, felt, or canvas with interfacing for stiffness. **Variations:** Add sequins, appliqué stars, or make reversible.

Steps:

1. Cut a long strip of fabric (20" x 6"). Add interfacing for sturdiness.

2. Cut a crown shape along one long edge (points or curves).

3. Sew lining and outer fabric right sides together, leaving opening.

4. Turn right side out and topstitch edges.

5. Add Velcro closure at back for adjustable fit.

Project 5: Play Mat

Fabric Suggestions: Cotton, flannel, or canvas. Add batting for a quilted version.

Variations: Create themed mats (roads, farm, park, or fairy tale world) with appliqué or fabric paint.

Steps:

1. Cut fabric rectangle 36" x 36".
2. Optional: Add batting and backing fabric for quilted effect.
3. Quilt layers together with straight-line stitching.
4. Hem or bind edges.
5. Decorate with appliqué shapes or fabric paint designs.

CHAPTER EIGHT

Eco-Friendly Sewing

Sewing is not only creative but can also support a greener lifestyle. With just one yard of fabric, you can make everyday reusable items that replace single-use plastics and paper. These projects are practical, washable, and make thoughtful gifts for eco-conscious friends.

Project 1: Reusable Grocery Bag

Fabric Suggestions: Sturdy cotton, canvas, denim, or duck cloth. **Variations:** Add a pocket, make foldable with a button closure, or sew with waterproof fabric for extra durability.

Steps:

1. Cut two rectangles (18" x 20") for the bag body.
2. Cut two strips (22" x 4") for handles.
3. Place rectangles right sides together and sew along sides and bottom.
4. Box the corners for a flat base (optional).
5. Hem the top edge.
6. Fold handle strips lengthwise, sew, turn right side out, and attach to bag.

Project 2: Produce Bags

Fabric Suggestions: Lightweight cotton, mesh, or muslin. **Variations:** Add a drawstring closure, label with size, or use different colors for fruits/vegetables.

Steps:

1. Cut fabric rectangles (12" x 16" or adjust as desired).
2. Fold in half lengthwise, right sides together.

3. Sew along side and bottom.

4. Hem top edge, leaving casing for drawstring.

5. Insert cord or ribbon for closure.

Project 3: Fabric Napkins

Fabric Suggestions: Cotton, linen, or flannel.

Variations: Use contrasting thread for decorative stitching, add embroidered initials, or make reversible napkins.

Steps:

1. Cut fabric squares (18" x 18").
2. Press ½" hem around all sides.
3. Fold raw edge under again to enclose, press.
4. Stitch along folded edges.
5. Optional: Add decorative stitching or embroidery.

Project 4: Coffee Cup Sleeve

Fabric Suggestions: Cotton with batting or felt lining for insulation. **Variations:** Add Velcro or button closure, use quilted fabric, or personalize with embroidery.

Steps:

1. Trace a template from a disposable coffee sleeve.
2. Cut two fabric pieces and one batting piece using template.
3. Layer fabric (right sides together) with batting on top.
4. Sew around edges, leaving opening.
5. Turn right side out, topstitch edges.
6. Add Velcro or button/loop for closure.

Project 5: Reusable Sandwich Wrap

Fabric Suggestions: Cotton lined with food-safe waterproof fabric (like PUL).

Variations: Make larger for wraps or smaller for snacks; add Velcro or ties.

Steps:

1. Cut one 12" x 12" square of cotton and one waterproof lining.

2. Place fabrics wrong sides together.

3. Bind edges with bias tape.

4. Attach Velcro strips or ribbon ties at two corners.

5. Fold around sandwich and secure.

CHAPTER NINE

Seasonal & Holiday Projects

Holidays and seasonal events are the perfect time to showcase your creativity with handmade decorations and gifts. With just one yard of fabric, you can stitch up festive items that bring warmth, charm, and a personal touch to any celebration.

Project 1: Christmas Stockings

Fabric Suggestions: Cotton, flannel, felt, or velvet. Add batting for a quilted look.

Variations: Make patchwork stockings, add names with embroidery, or use faux fur for cuffs.

Steps:

1. Create a stocking template (about 16" tall).
2. Cut two fabric pieces and two lining pieces.
3. Place outer fabric pieces right sides together; sew along edges, leaving top open.
4. Repeat with lining fabric.
5. Insert lining inside outer stocking.
6. Add cuff, loop for hanging, and finish edges.

Projct 2: Fabric Ornaments

Fabric Suggestions: Cotton, felt, or metallic holiday fabric.
Variations: Make stars, hearts, or trees; embellish with beads, sequins, or embroidery.

Steps:

1. Trace ornament shapes onto paper (star, tree, circle).
2. Cut two fabric pieces per ornament.
3. Place right sides together, sew around, leaving a small opening.

4. Turn right side out, stuff lightly, and stitch closed.

5. Attach ribbon loop for hanging.

Project 3: Halloween Trick-or-Treat Bag

Fabric Suggestions: Cotton, canvas, or felt for sturdiness.
Variations: Use glow-in-the-dark fabric paint, add appliqué pumpkins, bats, or ghosts.

Steps:

1. Cut two rectangles (14" x 16") for the bag body.

2. Cut two strips (18" x 3") for handles.

3. Sew sides and bottom of bag, right sides together.

4. Hem the top edge.

5. Attach handles to bag.

6. Decorate with appliqué or fabric paint.

Project 4: Easter Basket Liner

73

Fabric Suggestions: Cotton in pastel or spring prints.

Variations: Add lace trim, embroidery, or make reversible.

Steps:

1. Measure inside of basket: base diameter + height + 4".
2. Cut a circle for base and a wide strip for sides.
3. Sew strip into a ring; attach to circular base.

4. Hem top edge, leaving casing for ribbon.

5. Insert ribbon and tie in a bow.

Project 5: Table Centerpiece Runner

Fabric Suggestions: Cotton, linen, or festive holiday fabric.

Variations: Add batting for quilted runner, decorate with appliqué leaves, stars, or seasonal motifs.

Steps:

1. Cut fabric rectangle to desired length (12" x 36" or longer).
2. Cut backing fabric the same size.
3. Place right sides together, sew around edges, leaving opening.
4. Turn right side out, press flat, and topstitch edges.
5. Optional: Add decorative stitching or appliqué designs.

CHAPTER TEN

Upcycling & Creative Remixes

One of the joys of sewing is giving new life to old or leftover fabric. Instead of throwing away worn-out clothes, curtains, or small scraps, you can transform them into fresh, functional, and stylish pieces. This chapter focuses on creative upcycling — showing how to turn what you already have into something new and beautiful.

Tips for Upcycling & Repurposing Fabric

- **Look for sturdy textiles:** Old jeans, canvas totes, or curtains work well for structured projects.

- **Mix textures:** Combining cotton, denim, flannel, and lace creates a unique handmade look.

- **Use scraps smartly:** Save small pieces for appliqué, quilting, or accent details.

- **Check condition:** Avoid fabrics that are overly worn, stretched, or weak at the seams.

- **Prewash before sewing:** Especially when mixing different fabrics, to prevent shrinkage later.

Project 1: Patchwork Tote

Fabric Suggestions: Denim, cotton, or canvas scraps.

Variations: Make a quilted version, add a pocket, or stitch decorative embroidery on panels.

Steps:

1. Cut fabric scraps into squares (6" x 6") or rectangles.

2. Arrange in a patchwork design.

3. Sew squares together into two large panels (front and back).

4. Cut lining fabric to match.

5. Sew panels together, add lining, and attach handles.

Project 2: Quilted Pillow

Fabric Suggestions: Mixed cotton or flannel   scraps.

Variations: Try a geometric pattern (strips, triangles, or squares) or make it reversible.

Steps:

1. Cut scraps into desired shapes (squares, strips, or triangles).
2. Arrange into quilt top design.
3. Sew pieces together, pressing seams flat.
4. Add batting and backing fabric, quilt as desired.
5. Sew quilted front to pillow back with envelope or zipper closure.

Project 3: Scrap Fabric Coasters

Fabric Suggestions: Cotton, denim, or felt scraps.

Variations: Try round, square, or hexagon shapes; add appliqué or hand stitching for decoration.

Steps:

1. Cut fabric scraps into squares (5" x 5").
2. Cut batting or felt the same size.
3. Layer two fabric pieces with batting inside.
4. Sew around edges, leaving a small opening.
5. Turn right side out, topstitch to close and finish.

Project 4: Fabric Bunting/Garland

Fabric Suggestions: Cotton scraps in coordinating colors or prints.
Variations: Try triangles, rectangles, or scalloped shapes; use seasonal fabrics for holidays.

Steps:

1. Cut fabric into desired shapes (triangles work well, 6" tall).

2. Sew two pieces together, right sides facing, then turn right side out (or leave edges raw for a rustic look).
3. Press flat.
4. Sew shapes along a long bias tape or ribbon, evenly spaced.
5. Hang as festive décor.

Project 5: Mixed-Fabric Scarf

Fabric   Suggestions: Lightweight cotton, silk, chiffon, or knit scraps. **Variations:**   Make   patchwork-style strips, use fringed denim for a casual look, or alternate textures.

Steps:

1. Cut fabric strips of equal width (6" x 20").
2. Sew strips together lengthwise until desired scarf length is reached.
3. Press seams flat.
4. Hem all edges or leave raw for a frayed look.
5. Optional: Add tassels or fringe on ends.

CHAPTER ELEVEN

Finishing Touches & Personalization

The difference between a simple project and a standout handmade piece is often in the finishing details. Whether it's a touch of lace, a hand-stitched monogram, or a playful button closure, personalization transforms your one-yard creations into treasures that reflect your style — or the personality of someone you're gifting them to. This chapter explores fun ways to add character and flair to your sewing projects.

Adding Trims, Appliqué, and Embroidery

Fabric Suggestions: Cotton, linen, or any sturdy base fabric that can support embellishment.

Variations: Use lace for elegance, rickrack for a vintage vibe, or embroidery for a handmade touch.

Tips & Techniques:

1. **Trims:** Sew ribbon, lace, pom-poms, or ruffles along edges of bags, napkins, and clothing.
2. **Appliqué:** Cut out shapes from scraps, fuse with iron-on adhesive, then topstitch around edges.
3. **Embroidery:** Add initials, flowers, or borders using simple stitches like backstitch or French knots.

Using Fabric Paint, Iron-Ons, and Patches

Fabric Suggestions: Light- to medium-weight cotton or canvas for smooth surfaces.
Variations: Create bold designs with stencils, add iron-on vinyl quotes, or repair old fabric with colorful patches.

Tips & Techniques:

1. **Fabric Paint:** Use stencils, stamps, or freehand painting for designs. Heat-set with an iron.
2. **Iron-Ons:** Position design, cover with pressing cloth, and fuse with hot iron.
3. **Patches:** Sew or iron fun shapes over holes or as accents.

Creative Closures (Buttons, Snaps, Velcro, Ties)

Fabric Suggestions: Depends on project; heavier fabrics may need reinforced closures.

Variations: Choose closures to match style — elegant buttons, easy Velcro for kids, rustic ties, or magnetic snaps for bags.

Tips & Techniques:

1. **Buttons:** Mark placement, sew securely, and reinforce buttonholes.
2. **Snaps:** Use snap pliers or sew-on snaps for bags and pouches.
3. **Velcro:** Great for kids' items and quick fastening. Sew around edges for durability.
4. **Ties:** Sew fabric strips or ribbons into seams for wrap skirts, aprons, or gift bags.

Tips for Customizing Gifts & Making Projects Unique

- **Monograms:** Embroider or applique initials on bags, napkins, or pillow covers.
- **Color Themes:** Choose fabrics and trims that match the recipient's favorite colors or décor.
- **Mix & Match:** Combine multiple techniques — a painted tote with embroidered trim, or a scarf with appliquéd accents.

- **Packaging:** Present handmade gifts wrapped in fabric scraps or tied with coordinating ribbon.

CHAPTER TWELVE

Sewing Tips for Every Skill Level

No matter where you are in your sewing journey, every project brings new opportunities to learn. Mistakes happen, shortcuts save time, and sometimes you need to adapt a pattern to fit your needs. This chapter provides practical guidance to help you troubleshoot, adjust, and keep your sewing experience enjoyable.

Common Mistakes and How to Avoid Them

1. Skipped Stitches: Often caused by a dull or wrong-sized needle. Solution: Change needles regularly and match the type to your fabric.

2. **Uneven Seams:** Caused by fabric slipping or rushing. Solution: Use pins or clips and sew at a steady pace.

3. **Puckering Fabric:** Usually from incorrect thread tension. Solution: Test tension on a scrap before sewing your project.

4. **Fraying Edges:** Raw fabric edges unravel. Solution: Finish seams with zigzag stitching, pinking shears, or a serger.

5. **Pattern Cutting Errors:** Skipping notches or misaligning grain. Solution: Always double-check pattern placement before cutting.

Quick Fixes When Things Go Wrong

- **Broken Needle Mid-Project:** Replace needle and carefully backstitch to secure the seam where you left off.

- **Seam Ripped Too Far:** Reinforce by overlapping stitches slightly past the tear.

- **Crooked Stitching:** Use a seam ripper carefully, then re-sew slowly.

- **Fabric Too Short:** Add a contrasting fabric border or use piecing to extend.

- **Misaligned Hems:** Add trim or decorative stitching to disguise.

How to Scale Patterns Up or Down for Larger/Smaller Projects

1. **Enlarge/Reduce Templates:** Photocopy or scan patterns at a percentage larger/smaller.

2. **Grid Method:** Draw a grid over your pattern, then redraw it larger or smaller on graph paper.

3. **Proportion Adjustments:** When changing size, adjust seam allowances and placement of details (like pockets).

4. **Fabric Needs:** Scaling up often requires more fabric than one yard consider patchwork solutions.

Time-Saving Shortcuts for Busy Sewists

- **Chain Sewing:** Feed multiple pieces through machine one after another without cutting thread.
- **Press as You Go:** Saves time later by reducing wrinkled seams.
- **Pre-Cut Fabric:** Cut multiple projects in one sitting to streamline sewing time.
- **Batch Work:** Do all cutting, pressing, or stitching steps for multiple projects at once.
- **No-Pin Sewing:** For straight seams, skip pinning and guide fabric carefully by hand.

CONCLUSION

Your One-Yard Sewing Journey

With just a single yard of fabric, you've discovered how many stylish, practical, and meaningful projects you can create. From accessories and home décor to gifts, holiday treasures, and upcycled favorites, each stitch has shown that sewing doesn't have to be complicated to be rewarding.

As you continue your sewing journey, remember that every project is a chance to learn, express yourself, and add beauty to everyday life. Don't be afraid to experiment, personalize, and make each creation uniquely yours.

Most of all enjoy the process, celebrate your progress, and let your one-yard projects inspire a lifetime of creativity.

Printed in Dunstable, United Kingdom

71546660R00058